C++

Step-by-Step Guide to C++ Programming from Basics to Advanced

Robert Anderson

TABLE OF CONTENT

Chapter 1: Introduction and Installation

History of C++

C++ is a general purpose programming language. It's aim as a programming language is to offer a platform to create efficient and bare-boned applications. C++ was released in 1983, and first started on in 1979 by Bjarne Stroustrup where it was known as "C with classes" where it was later in 1983 renamed to be C++.

The language is still maintained with updates every few years, where it is still one of the most popular languages in the world.

Running C++ on Windows

One of the best ways to run C++ on a Windows based computer is Visual Studio, this can be downloaded directly from Microsoft with the most recent version being Visual Studio 2017.

Download and run the installer, throughout the installer you'll be met with this menu, make sure C++ is selected.

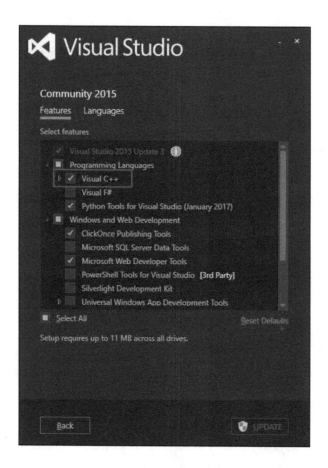

Complete the install and load up Visual Studio.

To create a project you need to then select FILE -> NEW PROJECT like so:

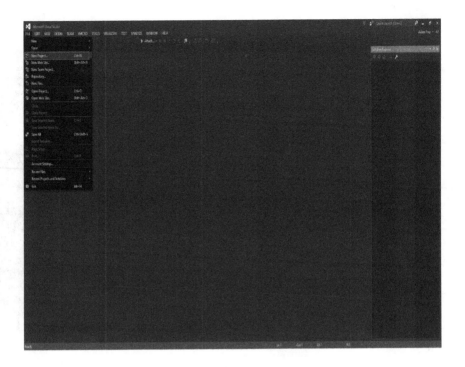

You'll then be met with this window:

Follow the menus through and you'll be ready to run the code.

Running C++ on Mac and Linux

Running on C++ on UNIX based environments can be achieved by the use of clang or "gcc", you can use it like so in the OS's terminal window:

```
gcc main.cpp -o main.out
```

The file can now be run like:

```
./main.out
```

You can create a .cpp file in a notepad editor of your choice.

Running C++ Online

A easy way to compile C++ online is by using "TutorialPoints" C++ Online, like is below:

https://www.tutorialspoint.com/compile_cpp11_online.php

And should look something like this:

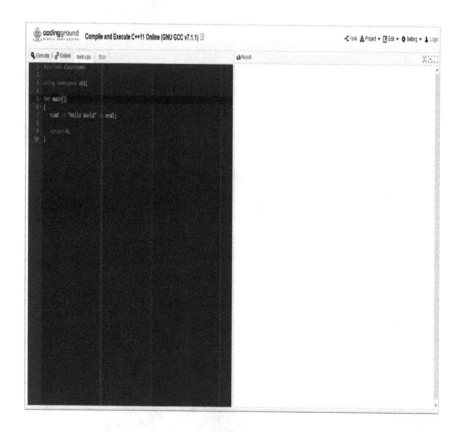

Prerequisite

A few things need to be explained before starting is basics:

The first is the basic program design:

```
#include "stdafx.h"

using namespace std;

int main()
{
    return 0;
}
```

The program above is the basic design provided, the code goes in the curly brackets of the main() section and each aspect will be described in the later sections.

You'll also come across lines that start with "//", these are comments and their only purpose is to add descriptions to label and explain code, they are defined by a distinctive green colour:

```
//Comment
```

The next thing is output from a program, in examples in upcoming chapters you will come across lines like:

```
cout << "Print" << endl;
```

This for the time being is simply printing out data to the screen, the sections of it will be explained in later sections.

Chapter 2: Basics

Variables and types

The basis of a program is data, in the form of numbers and characters. The storing, manipulation and output of this data gives functionality. Variables hold this data, think of it as a box used to store a single item.

C++ is a heavily typed language where each variable must have a defined type. A type is an identifying keyword that defines what the variable can hold. The first type we will come across is the integer, this can hold real numbers (numbers without a decimal place), an integer is defined below:

```
int value = 6;
```

- **int** is the defined type keyword, we will learn about the difference possibilities later.

- **"value"** is the ID for the variable, this can be anything you want to call it, this is used to allow a variable to have a meaningful name, the variable could be defined as **"int pineapple = 3;"**, but it's good practise to make them relevant. However, there are a few exception to this as a variable cannot be a single digit i.e. '4' or cannot contain special characters (!"£$ %^&*) etc.

- **"= 6;"** Is the assignment section, where the values of 3 is placed in the integer box for use later. **This also ends with a semi colon, this is used to signify the end of a line.**

This variable can now be used in valid areas of the program, like so:

```
int anotherValue = value;
```

The value of **"value"** defined earlier will now be placed in the **anotherValue** variable and they will now both have the value of 3. The value of **value** doesn't change as it is just being copied and placed into **anotherValue**.

String

The String is another crucial variable, this variable type is used to store a series of characters, an example could be the word "batman", the word is composed of characters that are stored in the String variable. It's an array of characters (More on arrays later), but effectively it's the single characters of the word stored next to each other in memory. The '\n' is a special character that stands for a newline.

```
#include "stdafx.h"

#include <string>
```

```cpp
using namespace std;

int main()
{
    //String class
    string wordStr = "";

    //Character array
    char wordCharArray[] = "";

    return 0;
}
```

As you can see above there are two ways to save a string, the first way is by using a 'wrapper' that is something that hides functionality and adds extra on top, this makes it easier to move around a string (we'll talk about passing around variables later) and the second way is to use a char array, string is the recommended way to store a string variables.

Note the use of:

```cpp
#include <string>
```

This informs the program you want to use the "string" wrapper in the program.

Boolean

Booleans are used as expressions, their values can only be **true** or **false** and are used to signify certain states or flag certain events, they can also hold the result for a conditional expression (More on conditional expressions later). These will make more sense when we go thought conditional statements.

```
bool True = true;
bool False = false;
```

Float/Double

Floating point variables are decimal values created with float point precision math, the technical elements of how this works are outside of the scope of this tutorial but can easily be explained through resources on the internet, just search "floating point precision". Floats allows for a higher level of accuracy of a value by providing decimal precision. You can specify a 'float' value by putting an 'f' and the end of the value.

```
float decimalValue = 3.0f;
```

Void

This data type is special and is used to specify no value is available. This sounds counter intuitive, but we'll see where this is used later.

Notable keywords/terms

const – This keyword turns the variable read-only, meaning it's value cannot be changed after it is initialised. The keyword is used like so:

```
const float pi = 3.14f;
```

Global variable – This is a term describing a variable definition outside the main function. For example, the **int** friendCount is a global variable and the **int** currentMonth is not. Note the positions they're defined:

```
//Global
int friendCount = 0;

int main()
{
        //Not Global
        int currentMonth = 5;


        return 0;
}
```

This means the global variable can be used in **any** location in the program and can be dangerous if not used correctly. One correct way it to use it in conjunction with the **const** keyword above, this means functions can only reference the value and not change it.

Recap

- int   Holds real numbers

- float / double   Hold decimal numbers

- void   Specifies there is not type

- boolean   Holds either true or false

- string   An array of characters making up a word or sentence

- global   A variable that can be accessed anywhere

- const   Means after a variable has been initialised its value cannot be changed

Conditionals

If statement

There are situations where you need something to happen if a certain condition is the case, this is the role of the If statement and where conditional statements come into the mix.

```
if (Condition)
```

```
{
        //Code will run here if Condition is true

}
//Code will jump here if Condition is false
```

In use:

```cpp
#include "stdafx.h"
#include <iostream>

using namespace std;

int main()
{
        int numberOfBooks = 10;
        if (numberOfBooks > 0)
        {
                cout << "You have a book!" << endl;
        }
}
```

Output:

> You have a book!

These allow a programmer to control the flow of the program and choose situations to happen when a possibility is true, we'll go onto more examples later.

Else Statement

Else's are optional but these can be added to the end of an if-statement and will only run if the if-statement condition is false

```
if (Condition)

{

    //Code will run here if Condition is True

}

else

{

    //Code will run here if Condition is False

}
```

Else statements can also become an else/if statement where a new if statement is attached, this look like this:

```
if (Condition1)
```

```
{

    //Code will run here if Condition1 is True

}

if else(Condition2)

{

    //Code will run here if Condition1 is False and Condition2 is True

}

//If neither are true no code will run
```

You can also chain another else statement onto an else statement effectively creating an infinite chain. If any conditions along the chain are true, the ones below are not checked, I'll demonstrate this below:

```
#include "stdafx.h"
#include <iostream>

using namespace std;

int main()
{
        if (false)
        {
                cout << "Contition1!" << endl;
```

```
        }
    else if (true) //This condition is true!
    {
            cout << "Contition2!" << endl;
    }
    else if (true) //Ignored, due to previous else statement being true
    {
            cout << "Contition3!" << endl;
    }
    else if (true) //Also ignored due to condition 2 being true
    {
            cout << "Contition4!" << endl;
    }

    return 0;
}
```

Output

> Condition 2

After the body of condition 2 is hit and the **cout** statement is executed, the program does not go onto to check the other else statements.

Exercise

Adapt a program to check if a value is equal to another and print "EQUAL", if they're not print "NOT EQUAL", the skeleton code is below:

```cpp
#include "stdafx.h"
#include <iostream>

using namespace std;

int main()
{
        int value1 = 10;
        int value2 = 10;


        //CODE GOES HERE
}
```

Solution

```cpp
#include "stdafx.h"
#include <iostream>

using namespace std;
```

```
int main()
{
        int value1 = 10;
        int value2 = 10;

        if (value1 == value2)
        {
                cout << "EQUAL";
        }
        else
        {
                cout << "NOT EQUAL";
        }

        return 0;
}
```

Change the values of value1 and value2 and see how the program changes.

Using multiple conditions

You can use more than one condition in a single statement, there're two ways of doing this **AND** signified by **&&** and **OR** signified by **||** (Double vertical bar).

AND checks if both conditions are true before triggering the body of the statement

```
if (Condition1 && Condition2)

{

    //Code will run here if Condition1 AND Condition2 are True

}
```

OR checks if one of the conditions are true before triggering the body of the statement

```
if (Condition1 || Condition2)

{

    //Code will run here if Condition1 OR Condition2 are True (Works
if both are true)

}
```

Recap

- If statement   Deals with conditional statements, code within it's body will run if the condition is true

- else statement   Used as an extension to an if statement that is only checked if the if statement is false

- &&   Used to string two conditions together and will only return true if both are true

- || (Double Bar) Used to string two conditions together and will only return true if one of the conditions are true

Switch-Case

Switch cases are used to test a variable for equality with a constant expression without the need for multiple if-statements. One use for this structure is check users input string. Below is the basic structure of the switch case:

```
//Switch-Case
switch (expression)
{
//Case statement
case constant-expression:
        break; //Break isn't needed

//Any number of case statements
// |
// |
//\ /
```

```
// .

default:
        break;
}
```

The switch starts off with an 'expression', this is the variable that is to be compared to the 'constant-expressions', these constants are the literal values of the variable such as '1' or 'Z'. Breaks are optional but without them the code will 'flow-down' into other statements. There is an example below using a switch-case statement, the user inputs a character if the char is N or Y, 'No' and 'Yes' is output respectively but there's a default case that applies for all situations, this needs to be at the end.

```
char character;

//Reads in user input (Explained in more detail later)
scanf("%s", &character);

        //Switch-Case
switch (character)
{
        case 'N':
                printf("NO\n");
                break;
        case 'Y':
```

```
            printf("YES\n");
            break;
    default:
            printf("Do not understand!\n");
            break;
}
```

If there is no **break** statement a 'flow-down' will occur, below is an example just like above but without the break statements and we'll what the output is like:

```
char character;


//Reads in user input (Explained in more detail later)
char character;
cin >> character;


//Switch-Case
switch (character)
{
    case 'N':
            printf("NO\n");
    case 'Y':
            printf("YES\n");
    default:
            printf("Do not understand!\n");
}
```

If 'N' is the user input the Output will be:

```
>NO

>YES

>Do not understand!
```

This is because when one case statement is triggered it will continue down until a break statement is found to stop running the case body code.

Iteration

Iteration means looping, and looping quickly gives programs the ability to perform lots of similar operations very quickly, there're two types of iteration: 'for loops' and 'while loops/do-while loop'

For Loop

The for loop is given an end value and loops up until that value, while keeping track of what loop number it's currently on, here is an example below:

```
for (int x = 0; x > 10; x++)
{
        cout << "Loop!" << endl;
}
```

```
for(int x = 0; x > 10; x++)
```

Each part of the for-loop has a role

Red

This is the *Declaration* section to define the loop counter variable, this defines the start point of the counter

Green

This section is called the *Conditional* and it contains a conditional statement that is checked at the end of the loop to see if the if-statement should continue looping, so in this case the loop should continue looping if **x > 10,** if this condition becomes false the loop will not continue.

Blue

The blue statement is the *Increment* section where the loop counter is incremented (increased in value), the **x++** is shorthand for **x = x + 1**. This can also be **x--**, if there was a case requiring the counter to decrease.

- Declaration section defines the loop counter

- Conditional section continues the loop if true

- Increment section is where the loop counter is incremented

Conditional Loops

Conditional loops work like the for loop but don't have a loop counter and will only loop while a condition is True. This means you can create an infinite loop, like so:

```
while (true)
{
        cout << "This will never stop looping!" << endl;
}
```

Note:

An infinite loop is normally constructed using a naked for-loop:

```
for (;;)
{
```

```
}
```

This loop will never end and your program will get stuck within the loop.

The example below shows if the condition is false the program will never reach the code within the brackets

```
while (false)
{
        cout << "This will never loop!" << endl;
}
```

To use this loop effectively you can use it with a conditional statement (like the if statement) or you can use it with a bool variable, examples are below

```
int count = 0;
while (count > 10)
{

        //Remember this, it's the same as "count = count + 1;"
        count++;
}
```

As it says above you can also use a while loop directly with a Boolean variable:

```
int count = 0;
bool keepLooping = true; //Bool is true (1) is true
while (keepLooping)
{
        //Remember this, it's the same as "count = count + 1;"
        count++;

        if (count == 3)
        {
                keepLooping = 0; //keepLooping is now false, and the
loop will stop
        }
}
```

Note:

The section in the brackets of the while loop is checking if that condition is true, you can also write it like so:

```
while (!stopLooping) {}
```

This is effectively saying, keep looping while stopLooping is "not true", the "!" is symbol means "not".

Do-While

A Do-While loop is almost exactly the same as While loop but with one small difference, it checks if the condition is true after executing the code in the body of the loop, a while loop checks the if the condition is true before executing the body. The code snippet below shows this difference:

```
while (false)
{
        cout << "While Loop" << endl;
}


do
{
        cout << "Do Loop" << endl;
} while (false)
```

Output:

> Do Loop

Because even though the Boolean is false, the Do loop executed a single time because the check was at the end of the body.

Using a Do-Loop

A real-world example of a do-loop cool be checking for user input, it prints out and asks for input if all is okay there is no need for looping if not it will loop. An example looking for the user to enter a 'a' is below

```
#include "stdafx.h"
#include <iostream>

using namespace std;

int main()
{
        //Will loop if this is false
        bool correct = true;
        do
        {
                cout << "Please enter the letter 'a':";

                //Takes in user input
                char a;
                cin >> a;
```

```cpp
        //Checks if answer is correct
        if (a != 'a')
        {
                //Incorrect
                correct = false;

                cout << "Incorrect" << endl;
        }
        else
        {
                //Correct
                correct = true;
        }
    } while (!correct);

    //If the user has completed the task
    cout << "Correct" << endl;
}
```

Loop control keywords

Sometimes there are situations where you want to prematurely stop the entire loop or a single iteration (loop), this is where loop control keywords come into use.

You have either a **break** or **continue** keyword

break – Will stop the entire loop, this can be useful if an answer has been found and the rest of the planned iterations would be pointless.

```
for (int x = 0; x < 5; x++)
{
        if (x == 3)
        {
                break;
        }

        //The technicalities of this statement will be explained later
        cout << "Loop value: " << x << endl;
}
```

Output:

> Loop value: 0

> Loop value: 1

> Loop value: 2

Now if the code is changed to not include the break:

```
for (int x = 0; x < 5; x++)
{
        //The technicals of this statement will be explained later
        cout << "Loop value: " << x << endl;

}
```

Output:

> Loop value: 0

> Loop value: 1

> Loop value: 2

> Loop value: 3

> Loop value: 4

Continue – If we use the code from above but replace it for a **continue** the code will look like so:

```
for (int x = 0; x < 5; x++)
{
        if (x == 3)
```

```
        {
                continue;
        }

        //The technicals of this statement will be explained later
        cout << "Loop value: " << x << endl;
}
```

The output it like so:

```
Output:

> Loop value: 0

> Loop value: 1

> Loop value: 2

> Loop value: 4
```

This shows that when *x = 3* the **continue** is executed and the loop is skipped and so is the **cout** statement is also skipped so there is no "Loop value: 3"

Nested loops

You can also place loops within loops to perform specific roles, in the example we are using for-loops but this can also be done with the while/do loop.

The example is printing out a 2D grid, the nested for-loop gives another dimension:

```
//Prints a 5x5 grid
for (int y = 0; y < 5; y++)
{
        for (int x = 0; x < 5; x++)
        {
                //Prints an element of the row
                cout << "X ";
        }

        //Moves down a row
        cout << endl;
}
```

Output

> X X X X X

> X X X X X

> X X X X X

> X X X X X

Functions

Functions are the building blocks of a program, they allow the reuse of code, the ability to keep it readable and stops the programmer repeating code. Repeating code is heavily advised against because bugs will be repeated multiple times and changes to code also need repeating. Functions give a centralised controlled area that deals with the distinct roles of the program.

A method has two elements, **parameters**:(the items passed into the function) and the **return type** (the variable being returned) these are both optional and you can have a function with neither.

A function must be defined above its call, like so;

```
//Function call
void PrintSmile()
{
        cout << ":)" << endl;
}
```

```
int main()
{
        //Method call
        PrintSmile();


        return 0;

}
```

Function Parameters

Sometimes it might be useful to pass data into a program, there are two types of parameter passing, by **reference** and by **value.** Passing by reference is what it sounds like, it passes a direct reference to a variable not a copy, so any changes to that passed variable effect it back in the calling function. Passing by value is the passing of a copy of that variable, so any changes to that variable do not effect that passed variable.

- Passing by reference means changes to the parameter effects the passed variable

- Passing by value means changes to parameter does not affect the passed variable

Passing by value

```
void Add(int num1, int num2)
```

```
{
        //Adds values together
        int newValue = num1 + num2;


        //Prints result
        printf("The result is: %d", newValue);
}

int main()
{
        //Method call
        Add(10, 4);


        return 0;
}
```

Output:

> The result is: 14

Below is another example but this time a string is used a parameter:

```
void PrintStr(char word[])
{
        cout << word << endl;
```

```
}
```

The method call looks like this:

```
PrintStr("Flying Squirrel");
```

This is an incredibly useful feature that allows us to make general purpose code and change its function output by what is put in as a parameter.

Passing by reference

Passing by reference is done with the use of pointers (Will be further explained later) but a pointer is a memory address, so any changes done affect the variable being passed in. A reference parameter is shown by the "&" and is done like so:

```cpp
void Change(int& ParaValue)
{
        ParaValue = 20;
}


int main()
{
        int value = 10;

        Change(value);

        cout << value << endl;

        return 0;
}
```

Output

>20

As you can see the change method alters the value of the integer 'value' and effects the value back in the main method.

Returning values

Returning allows us to return data from a method, this lets us do computation within a function and get the function to automatically return the result. Let's take the one of the previous examples and adapt it so it returns the result instead of printing it:

```
int Add(int num1, int num2)
{
        //Adds values together
        int newValue = num1 + num2;


        //Returned keyword
        return newValue;
}

int main()
{
        //Method call
        int storeResult = Add(10, 4);


        return 0;
```

```
}
```

The areas that changed have been highlighted. When a value is to be returned, the "return" keyword is used, after this line has run it returns to the **line where the method was called** so any code under the return **will not run.**

The returned result is then stored in 'storeResult' to be used later. Returning can happen with any variable type. I'll show you an example below that checks if the number is an even value (Using the modulus operator talked about above that finds the remainder of a division):

```
bool EvenNumber(int value)
{
        if (value % 2 == 0)
        {
                //Return true
                return 1;
        }
        return 0;
}

int main()
{
        if (EvenNumber(2))
        {
```

```
                    cout << "Even number!" << endl;

        }

    if (EvenNumber(5))
        {
                    cout << "Odd number!" << endl;

        }

    return 0;
}
```

Output:

>Even number!

This program uses the return variable form the method EvenNumber() as a conditional for the if-statement and if it's true it will print "Even number!". As you can see from the output the first one prints but the second does not.

Arrays

Arrays have been mentioned previously, it is a data structure that holds a set number of variables next to each other in memory. The array will be given a *type*, for example 'int'. Arrays are used to quickly define lots of variables and keep relevant variables together. An array is defined below:

A static size, with the size in the square brackets:

```
int lotsOfNumber[20];
```

Or you can define values at the definition, **Note**: a size does not need to be defined because it's automatically determined by the number of values you specify:

```
int lotsOfNumbers[] = {1,3,4};
```

- **Arrays start at 0**, so the first index has an identifying value of 0, the second is 1 and so on. This means when accessing values, you need to remember it is always one less than the number of values it contains

You can access an index like so:

```
int var = lotsOfNumbers[0];
```

This will grab the first index of the array and place it in 'var'.

Arrays are very useful to access the tightly related data very quickly, you can use a for-loop to loop through the indexes and use them according. An example is below:

```
int lotsOfNumbers[] = { 1, 3, 4, 10};
for (int x = 0; x < 4; x++)
{
```

```
        cout << x << endl;

}
```

Output:

> 1

> 3

> 4

> 10

In C++ you cannot get the length directly and need to work it out, this can be done simply using the **sizeof()** keyword, this returns the size of the elements in the brackets, so for example on a 64bit machine a **int** should be represented using 4bytes so **sizeof** will return 4. The length of an array can be worked out as so:

```
int arrayLength = sizeof(lotsOfNumbers) / sizeof(lotsOfNumbers[0]);
```

This takes the entire size of the array, and divides it by the first element and the division gives how many indices the array holds.

Multi-dimensional arrays

You can also define a second dimension in the array or even a third, this gives more flexibility when working with arrays. For example, a 2D array could be used to store coordinates or positions of a grid. A 2D array is defined as so:

```
int arrayOfNumbers[][2] = { {1,1}, {1,1}};
```

You access an element by putting the values in the square brackets for the x and y coordinate

```
int element = arrayOfNumbers[X][Y]
```

The obvious difference is that the second dimension **needs** a value, this cannot be automatically resolved when creating an array and that the initialization requires nested curly brackets. Below is the 3D example:

```
int arrayOfNumbers[][][2] = {{{1,1},{1,1}},{{1,1},{1,1}}};
```

But at this stage it is starting to lose readability and it's much better practise to lay it out like so:

```
int arrayOfNumbers[][][2] =
{
```

```
    {{1,1},{1,1}},
    {{1,1},{1,1}}
};
```

Passing Arrays in functions

As we saw when we learned about functions above, passing variables in as parameters can be very useful and so can passing in lots of variables stored as an array. However, we learnt above how to determine the size of an array above but this **does not work** with an array passed as a parameter, so we must pass in a variable that represents the number of elements that array is holding. There is a special variable type used to hold count variables, it's called **size_t** and it is an unsigned integer value (Meaning it cannot become negative) used to hold values for a count.

An example of an array being passed as a parameter is below:

```
void Print_SingleDimenArray(size_t length, int ageArray[])

{
        //Length is used to dynamically determine the for loop length
        for (int i = 0; i < length; i++)
        {
                printf("%d\n",ageArray[i]);
        }
```

```
}


int main()
{
        //An array of ages
        int ages[] = { 32, 11, 12, 1, 8, 5, 10 };

        //Size is determined as shown previously
        size_t ageLen = sizeof(ages) / sizeof(ages[0]);

        //Method call
        Print_SingleDimenArray(ageLen, ages);
}
```

Output
>32
>11
>12
>1
>8
>5
>10

The array has been passed and used to print values. The length of the array is crucial to the program as it allows the for loop to work for arrays of varying length.

- Any changes to an array in any method will change the array variable in the calling method. This is what was mentioned earlier as **passing by reference,** the whole array isn't copied and passed by reference with a little trickery occurring.

User I/O

There are situations and programming problems that involve the use of user interaction this is where user input and output comes in, the library that deals with this is known as "iostream" and is included into the project like:

```
#include <iostream>
```

Printing/Output

Sometimes the user needs a prompt or information needs to be displayed, this is where console printing comes into use, the key word **cout** is used to print out data to the screen, this is then used with the **stream insertion operator** that is written as "<<" this is used to signify what is to be printed. And example is below:

```
cout << "Hello!" << endl;
```

The output would just be the word "Hello!" to the screen. The **endl** is just used to print a carriage return ("**\n**")

You can also create an output involving a variable or another string, multiple stream insertion operators are used:

```
int x = 10;
cout << "The value is: " << x << endl;
```

Output

> The value is: 10

Reading/Input

Taking in user input can also be useful, the operator used is known as the **stream extraction operator** "**>>**" and is used in conjunction with **cin**, it works like so:

```cpp
#include "stdafx.h"
#include <iostream>

using namespace std;

int main()
{
        //Reads in name
        char name[10];
        cin >> name;

        //Prints name
        cout << name;
}
```

End of chapter Quiz

This section is designed to keep you on your toes about the previous content, there will be 10 questions that you can answer to test your knowledge, below in the neighbouring section will be the answers.

1. Name the data type used to hold a series of characters?'

2. What is the "%" sign used for?

3. What is this sign checking for "=="?

4. If a "&&" is between two conditional statements in a singular if, what does it mean?

5. What does "++" mean at the end of variable mean?

6. What is this operator called: ">>"?

7. Does an array have a built in property to find its size?

8. What is this loop called, and what does it do?

```
for(;;)

{



}
```

9. What two values does a Boolean variable hold?

10. Where is the type 'void' used?

Answers

1. String.

2. Gets the modular of two numbers.

3. If the two values either side are equal.

4. That the statement will only be true if **both** of the conditionals are true.

5. It will increment the value of that variable.

6. The stream extraction operator.

7. No, the only way to find it is to use the **sizeof()** operator to find the total size of the array and each elements size, then divide both values to find the size.

8. It is called a naked for loop, and will just loop forever.

9. True or False.

10. Used when signifying a function does not return a value.

Chapter 3: Class Structure and OOP

Classes are the building blocks of a program in C++, they allow easy cookie cutter way of creating places that store and represent data. A class in C++ has two files, the header file (.h) and the implementation file (.cpp).

- Header file should just contain definitions of classes and variables.

- The implementation file as the name suggests contains the actual functionality of the functions and variables.

A header file looks like this when empty:

```
class Example
{
public:
        Example();
        ~Example();
};
```

There are some key bits about this, the **public** section defines how the methods can be accessed, don't worry too much about this yet as this will be explained further in the Encapsulation section. And the Example() and ~Example() functions are the Constructor and Destructor respectively, and the constructor runs when the class is created, and the destructor runs when the class is destroyed, this can either be done manually by calling the method or the compiler will do this automatically.

The .cpp file then looks like this:

```
#include "Example.h"

Example::Example()
{
}

Example::~Example()
{
}
```

Each of these are references to the Example's classes. You can implement functions or variables that are not defined in the header file, however this is considered a bad practice.

So for example lets used a fleshed out version of a class to show how it can be used. An example is below:

```
class Shape
```

```cpp
{
public:

        Shape(double len, double wid);

         ~Shape();


        double getArea();


private:

        double length;
        double width;
        double area;
};
```

```cpp
#include "Shape.h"
#include <iostream>
using namespace std;


Shape::Shape(double len, double wid)
{

        length = len;
        width = wid;


        area = length * width;


        cout << "Shape made!" << endl;

}
```

```
Shape::~Shape()
{
}


double Shape::getArea()
{
        return area;
}
```

And an instance of shape can be made like so:

```
Shape s = Shape(10, 10);
```

Note: the header file needs including at the top:

```
#include "Shape.h"
```

This gives the programmer a really easy way to create lots of containers for useful data.

Inheritance

Inheritance is one of the most important concepts in object orientated programming, it's the idea of taking a class, the base class and giving other classes it's characteristics like functions and variables. This provides a perfect opportunity to reuse code.

With our shape example above, we can now create another class called "Square" but we inherit characteristics from the base class "Shape". For displaying purposes I'm going to put all code into a single .cpp file from now on. The Square class is below:

```cpp
#include "stdafx.h"
#include <iostream>

using namespace std;



class Shape
{
public:
        double length;
        double width;
        double area;

        Shape(double l, double w)
        {
                length = l;
                width = w;
                area = l * w;
```

```cpp
        }
        ~Shape()
        {

        }
        double getArea()
        {
                return area;
        }

};

class Square : public Shape
{
public:
        Square(double l, double w) : Shape(l, w)
        {

        }
};

int main()
{
        Square s = Square(10, 10);
        cout << s.getArea() << endl;

}
```

Square now has everything that Shape has defined as Public and Protected (These will be explained in the next section) but as mentioned above it's a great way to repeat already created code.

Exercise

Add a class called "Rectangle" and let it inherit from the shape class. Don't forget to include a constructor for the rectangle class.

Solution

Something like this:

```cpp
class Rectangle : public Shape
{
public:
        Rectangle(double l, double w) : Shape(l, w)
        {

        }
};
```

Encapsulation

Encapsulation is the idea of limiting access to sensitive variables or methods contained within a class, there're three different access modifiers:

	Containing Class	Derived Class	Containing Assembly	Outside Assembly
Publ ic				
Prot ecte d				
Priva te				

Above is a grid comparing where you can and cannot access a variable or method marked with either modifier.

- Containing class is the class that the object was defined.

- Derived class is any class that inherits another

- Containing Assembly is anywhere inside the current .exe or .dll file

- Outside Assembly is any other area that exists

This means you can control the access to variables. But what if a variable is marked as private, what if it needs to be accessed externally? You used "getters" and "setters", methods that are specifically designed to retrieve and alter variables. These are a wonderful practise to keep code safe and secure, so let's alter our shape class to make it more secure.

Before we could do this:

```
Shape s = Shape(10,10);
s.length = -1;
```

This is undesirable as it invalid information, you cannot have a negative length, this is where a setter comes into use, the function can contain code to validate (check) the value that is attempting to be placed in the length variable, something like this:

```
void setLength(double value)
{
        if (value > 0)
        {
                length = value;
        }
        else
        {
                cout << "Error: Value is negative!" << endl;
        }
}
```

This function performs the necessary checks on the value to prevent invalid information getting into variables in the class. Below is an improved version of the class:

```cpp
class Shape
{
private:
        double length;
        double width;
        double area;


public:
        Shape(double l, double w)
        {
                length = l;
                width = w;
                area = l * w;
        }
        ~Shape()
        {

        }

        double getArea()
```

```
        {
                return area;
        }
        double getLength()
        {
                return length;
        }
        double getWidth()
        {
                return width;
        }
}
```

As you can see all the variables have been marked as Private and getters have been added, this is the way classes should be structure.

Polymorphism

The word polymorphism means having many forms and polymorphism in the context of OOP means having one method that can have many roles.

We can use the example of the class shape and overload a method that determines the area if for example we wanted to make a Triangle class, this is the shape class but with a virtual getArea() method:

```cpp
class Shape
{
protected:
        double length;
        double width;
        double area;

public:
        Shape(double l, double w)
        {
                length = l;
                width = w;
        }
        ~Shape()
        {


        }

        virtual double getArea()
        {
                return length * width;
        }
};
```

Virtual methods give the option be overridden an changed by a class that inherits it, it is also an optional change.

```cpp
class Triangle : public Shape
{
public:
        Triangle(double l, double w) : Shape(l, w)
        {

        }



        double getArea() override
        {
                return 0.5 * (length * width);
        }
};
```

Above is the implementation of the Triangle class, highlighted is the "override" keyword used to change the functionality of the virtual function.

```cpp
int main()
{
        Shape s = Shape(10, 10);
        cout << "The shapes area is: " << s.getArea() << endl;
```

```
        Triangle t = Triangle(10, 10);

        cout << "The triangles area is: " << t.getArea() << endl;
}
```

Ouput

>The shapes area is: 100

>The shapes area is: 50

As you can see from the example above each getArea() function is implemented differently and returns a different result.

This polymorphic design still gives the ease of creating lots of new data types without the need for repeating code but with a level of customising involved.

Exercise

Add a new class called Circle, it will need a different constrictor that only takes height and the getArea method needs overloading.

Solution

```
class Circle : public Shape
{
public:
        Circle(double h) : Shape(h, 0)
        {

        }

        double getArea() override
        {
                return 3.14 * ((length / 2) * (length / 2));
        }
};
```

As you can see a constructor is provided that only includes the height and the getArea() returns an relatively imprecise area for the circle.

Polymorphism if done correctly can give an extremely clean and readable code base with methods and classes adapting behaviour where necessary.

Interfaces

An interface describes the behaviour of capabilities of C++ class without committing to implementation. Interfaces are implemented using abstract classes, and are just the plan for the class.

Abstracts classes are made by adding a pure virtual functions to a class, a pure virtual function is a function with no body and is specified by placing a "=0" next to the function like so:

```
virtual double getVar() = 0;
```

This means the role the function is just to be inherited and adapted. Failing to override a pure virtual function in an inherited class results in an error, so It's considered a strict blueprint to design classes.

An error seen from not implementing a pure virtual function:

```
Dog d
object of abstract class type "Dog" is not allowed:
        pure virtual function "Animal::MakeSound" has no overrider
```

Below is an example involving animals:

```
#include "stdafx.h"
#include <iostream>

using namespace std;
```

```cpp
class Animal
{
public:
        //Pure virtual function
        virtual void MakeSound() = 0;
};

class Dog : public Animal
{
public:
        void MakeSound()
        {
                cout << "Bark!" << endl;
        }
};

class Cat : public Animal
{
public:
        void MakeSound()
        {
                cout << "Meow!" << endl;
        }
};

class Lion : public Animal
{
```

```cpp
public:
        void MakeSound()
        {
                cout << "Raw!" << endl;
        }
};

int main()
{
        Dog d;
        d.MakeSound();

        Cat c;
        c.MakeSound();

        Lion l;
        l.MakeSound();
}
```

Output

>Bark!

>Meow!

>Raw!

As you can tell it's a very rudimental pointless example, however it's supposed to show how a base class can hold basic information and class that inherits it is supposed to add information on top, in this example the program states that anything that inherits animals needs to have a sound, this can be adapted upon to make complex designs for classes and easily fill in relevant implementation.

Another example below will use the classic shape example and have a base class called "Shape" that will have an abstract function "getArea()" that will need implementing for each shape:

```cpp
#include "stdafx.h"
#include <iostream>

using namespace std;

class Shape
{
public:
        //Pure virtual function
        virtual int Area() = 0;

        Shape(double h, double w)
        {
                heigth = h;
```

```cpp
                width = w;
        }
protected:
        double heigth;
        double width;
};


class Circle : public Shape
{
public:
        Circle(double h, double w) : Shape(h, w) {}

        int Area()
        {
                return 3.14 * ((heigth / 2) * (heigth / 2));
        }
};

class Rectangle : public Shape
{
public:
        Rectangle(double h, double w) : Shape(h, w) {}

        int Area()
        {
                return heigth * width;
        }
};
```

```
int main()
{
        Rectangle r = Rectangle(10, 20);
        cout << r.Area() << endl;


        Circle c = Circle(5, 5);
        cout << c.Area() << endl;


}
```

Another simple example, but take your time and get used to it, abstract class architecture allows easy addition of new function and classes even if the design has been made due to the easy blueprint-esk design.

End of chapter Quiz

1. What are the two files used to make a class?

2. What symbol comes before the destructor definition?

3. What role should a header file take?

4. What does protected mean for a variable that is being inherited?

5. What is the role of polymorphism?

6. What keyword is used to change a virtual method?

7. How do you signify a pure virtual function?

8. Where can a function or variable marked as private be accessed?

9. What is role of the constructor?

10. What should the .cpp file contain?

Answers

1. Header (.h) and C++ file (.cpp).

2. The symbol "~" I used to show a destructor.

3. Just definitions of functions and variables.

4. It can only be accessed outside the definition class by a class that inherits it.

5. To have a single base definition but lots of different implementations.

6. Override is used to change a virtual method

7. With a normal function definition that is equal to zero.

8. Only in the class where it was defined.

9. Is a special function without a return type that is called when an instance of a class is created.

10. Implication of functions and variables defined in the header file.

Chapter 4: Improved Techniques

Structures

Structs originate from C, and come from the world of pre-class programming. However, they're still useful and can be use in places where classes are deemed as overkill.

A good example of using a structure being used can be for record keeping, for example you needed to keep track of football players in a team you would need to store:

- Name

- Kit Number

- Wage

- Strongest foot

- Etc

If there is no need to add functionality onto this information a structure is perfect for this situation. A structure storing this information is defined like this:

```
struct FootballPlayer
{
```

```
    string Name;
    int KitNumber;
    double Wage;
    string StrongestFoot;
};
```

This structure contains all the values that are relevant, this will provide a relevant container for similar information.

A new instance of the structure is defined like so:

```
FootballPlayer player1;
player1.Name = "Messi";
player1.KitNumber = 10;
player1.Wage = 1000000;
player1.StrongestFoot = "Both";
```

This code will create a FootballPlayer and assign values to all its member variables.

Real world usage of structures tend to be "simple" usage where they need to just store trivial data like the example above, when there needs to be functionality and encapsulation use a class. This is known a POD (Plain Old Data) encapsulation.

Note: The default access for structure variables is **public** while classes default to **private.**

Enums

Enums is short for Enumerated Type as has the role of a boolean but with unlimited user defined types, this can be used a flags for a situation like "HOME_SCREEN" or "SETTING_SCREEN".

An enum is defined like so:

```
enum CurrentScreen
{
        HOME,
        SETTINGS,
        CONTACTS,
        CALCULATOR
};
```

With each word in the brackets being a state the enum can be set as. A enum instance is created like so:

```
int main()
{
        CurrentScreen phone1;
```

```
        phone1 = HOME;
}
```

This code above makes a new enum and assigns it as "HOME". You can now use the enum to check what states it is, the example below will use a switch-case:

```
#include "stdafx.h"
#include <iostream>

using namespace std;

enum CurrentScreen
{
        HOME,
        SETTINGS,
        CONTACTS,
        CALCULATOR
};

int main()
{
        CurrentScreen phone1;
```

```cpp
//Change me
phone1 = HOME;

switch (phone1)
{
case HOME:
        cout << "You're on the home page" << endl;

        break;
case SETTINGS:
        cout << "You're on the settings page" << endl;

        break;
case CONTACTS:
        cout << "You're on the contacts page" << endl;

        break;
case CALCULATOR:
        cout << "You're on the calculator page" << endl;

        break;
default:
        break;
}

}
```

This code shows you can use conditional structures along with an enum to easily create a nice branched structure. Mess around with the commented "Change me" enum definition and see how the output changes.

Unions

Unions are a data structures designed to provide efficient memory usages, they can contain as many member variables as it needs however it can **only** store data for a **single variable** at a time. So the entire structure only takes up memory for the biggest member variable.

These have to be used with caution because setting value of another member variable will remove data stored in another, so it is incredibly easy to lose important data.

A union is defined like so:

```
union Example
{
```

```
        int i;

        int x;

        int y;

};
```

And an instance and value is created like so:

```
Example e;
e.i = 4;
```

To show how the size of the union works the program below works it through:

```
#include "stdafx.h"
#include <iostream>

using namespace std;

union Example
{
        int i;

        int x;

        int y;
```

```
};

int main()
{
        Example e;
        e.i = 4;

        cout << "Your int size is: " << sizeof(int) << " bytes" << endl;
        cout << "The union has 3 variables that should be a total of:  "
<< sizeof(int) * 3 << " bytes"<< endl;
        cout << "However, the union is " << sizeof(e) << " bytes" <<
endl;
}
```

Depending on your CPU architecture your output will be:

Ouput
>Your int size is: 4 bytes
>The union has 3 variables that should be a total of: 12 bytes
>However, the union is 4 bytes

As you can tell the union is only the size of a single integer, these structures can be used to efficiently use memory is there're situations where variables are idle and only one is needed.

Below is code that shows what happens to all the values when one is changed:

```cpp
#include "stdafx.h"
#include <iostream>

using namespace std;

union Example
{
        int i;
        int x;
        int y;
};

void Print_Union(Example e)
{
        cout << "i: " << e.i << endl;
        cout << "x: " << e.x << endl;
        cout <<          "y: " << e.y << endl;
}

int main()
{
        Example e;

        cout << "1" << endl;
        e.i = 4;
```

```
        Print_Union(e);

        cout << "2" << endl;
        e.y = 3;
        Print_Union(e);

        cout << "3" << endl;
        e.x = 1;
        Print_Union(e);
}
```

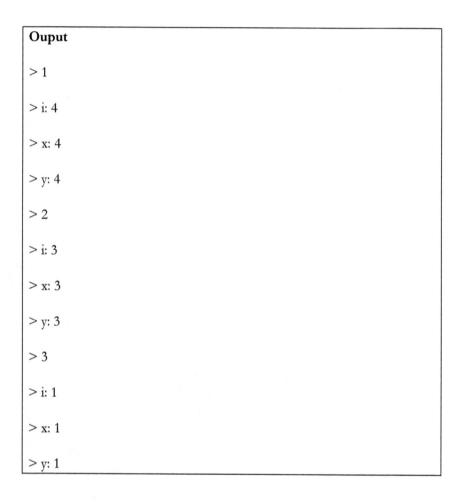

Ouput

> 1

> i: 4

> x: 4

> y: 4

> 2

> i: 3

> x: 3

> y: 3

> 3

> i: 1

> x: 1

> y: 1

As you can tell when you change one value, they all equal the same value, this is because all **values share the same memory location** and therefore when one changes they all change.

Variable argument lists

Variable argument lists allow for the possibly of endless parameters. Before we have come across functions with a static set amount of parameters (variables you can pass into a method) like:

```
int Add(int i, int y)
{

}
```

Has two parameters integer "i" and integer "y".

This is known as a **Variadic Function** or a function with unlimited **arity** (parameter number, so "Add" above has an arity of 2)

The variables are stored in a variable known as the **va_list** this works as any other variable but it just holds the list of variables passed. A variadic function is defined like so:

```
void Add(int numberOfVariables, ...)
{

}
```

Where "numberOfVariables" is the number of extra parameters passed, note this does not include this variable. This is required because the va_list does not know the total number of variables and does not keep track of where it is in the list.

Using the va_ist requires the use of a few functions:

- **va_start**(va_list, numberOfVariables)

    o Grabs the variables passed in and assigns the number specified by the second parameter to the first parameter

- **va_arg**(va_list, type)

    o Grabs the next variable from the specified list in the first parameter and creates a variable specified by "type"

- **va_end**(va_list)

    o Tidies up the list specified

We can now use these functions to create a working variadic function:

```cpp
#include "stdafx.h"
#include <cstdarg>
#include <iostream>

using namespace std;

void Add(int numberOfVariables, ...)
{
        //The variable list
        va_list arg;

        //Grabs the list
        va_start(arg, numberOfVariables);

        int total = 0;
        for (int i = 0; i < numberOfVariables; i++)
        {
                //Grabs the next variable
                total += va_arg(arg, int);
        }

        //Clean up
        va_end(arg);

        cout << "Total is: " << total << endl;
}
```

```
int main()
{
        //4 Arguments
        Add(4,
                1, 2, 3, 4);

        //10 Arguments
        Add(10,
                6, 9, 5, 11, 22, 1, 3, 56, 90, 63);
}
```

Ouput

>Total is: 10

>Total is: 266

Each section of the variable list process is labelled, this function adds all parameters it's given. This gives a very dynamic way to create one function that can handle an almost infinite list of parameters.

Exercise

Create a function that multiplies all the parameters given and returns a value, print out that value. Note: this #include is required:

```cpp
#include <cstdarg>
```

Solution

Something like this:

```cpp
#include "stdafx.h"
#include <cstdarg>
#include <iostream>

using namespace std;

int Multi(int numberOfVariables, ...)
{
    va_list arg;
    va_start(arg, numberOfVariables);

    int total = 1;
    for (int i = 0; i < numberOfVariables; i++)
    {
        //Grabs the next variable
        total *= va_arg(arg, int);
    }
    va_end(arg);

    return total;
```

```
}

int main()
{
        cout << "The total is: " << Multi(3, 56, 90, 63) << endl;
}
```

Namespaces

Namespaces are used to prevent variables and functions with the same name getting mixed up, for example the function Run() can be applicable in many situations so there needs to be a way to distinguish between different Run() functions, this is where namespaces can be used.

They are defined like so with all functions and variables in the curly brackets being part of that namespace:

```
namespace NamespaceName
{

}
```

The example below shows how they are used:

Two namespaces are defined like so with the same function name:

```
namespace Proccesing
{
        void Run()
        {
                cout << "Processing!" << endl;
        }
}


namespace Initialisation
{
        void Run()
        {
                cout << "Initialisation started!" << endl;
        }
}
```

This gives the programmer the opportunity to pick which Run() they can execute by just specifying the namespace like so:

```
Proccesing::Run();
```

and

```
Initialisation::Run();
```

and with them both run together:

```
int main()
{
        Initialisation::Run();
        Proccesing::Run();
}
```

Output

> Initialisation started!

> Processing!

Namespaces therefore gives a way to neatly segment code, and improves readability by providing a way to almost label blocks of code.

End of chapter Quiz

1. What is the recommended situation you should use a struct?

2. What is enum short for?

3. How the size of a union dictated?

4. What is a key factor about a union?

5. What is a Variadic function?

6. What does a va_list hold?

7. Why do you need to specified the number of parameters in a variable function?

8. Why does va_end() need to be run?

9. What is the base role of a namespace?

10. What syntax is used when calling a function inside a namespace, say you're calling the function Add() inside the namespace Math?

Answers

1. For plain old data (POD).

2. Enumerated type.

3. It's the size of its largest member variable

4. All the member variables share the same memory location so only on variable can hold a value at once

5. A function with a possibly unlimited number of parameters

6. A list of passed in variables to a function

7. There is no way to tell the size of a va_list, so you need to specify the number of passed parameters

8. It performs the clean-up of the variable list when it has been used

9. To segment and label variables and functions in a meaningful way.

10. Math::Add()

Chapter 5: Advanced Features

File I/O

You will eventually come across a programming situation where you need data to exist between the program running and not running, this is where file saving comes into use.

File saving is achieved by using functions in the **fstream** library, that is included like this:

```
#include <fstream>
```

You also need "iostream" that we've come across before for "cout" and "cin"

```
#include <iostream>
```

There are three main objects that are used when saving and reading to file:

- ofstream
    - This deals with the output stream, and is used to create and write data to a file

- ifstream

  - This is the opposite of ofstream and is used to read data from files

- fstream

  - This is a function that has the characteristic of both ofstream and ifstream.

Opening a file

To open a file we need to use the "open()" function that is a member of all the main objects, it works like so:

```
fstream f;
f.open("file.txt", ios::in);
```

Where:

- "file.txt" Is the filename

- "ios::in" is the flag for how the file is to be open, below is a table explaining all the options.

Name	Description
ios::app	Opens the file in append mode, all input is to be added to the end of the file
ios::ate	Opens a file for input into a file, and moves the read/write control to the

	end of the file
ios::in	Opens a file for reading
ios::out	Opens a file for writing
Ios::trunc	If the file exists, the data inside is deleted (truncated)

You can also have two of these modes by **OR**ing them together, this can be useful if you want to open the file to write to it and you want to get rid of already existing data:

```
f.open("file.txt", ios::out || ios::trunc);
```

Closing a file

Closing a file is as simple as you'd image. To achieve this all you need to call is the "close()" function:

```
f.close();
```

This flushes the stream and releases all the allocated memory to the file.

Writing to a file

Writing to a file is achieved by the use of the use of the insertion operator (<<), this has been met before in the case of "cout" and all that need to be done is data needs to be streams to a fsteam or ofstream instead of cout.

This is done like so:

```
f << "Writing data!" << endl;
```

Reading data

Reading data is the same as writing data, just flipped. You use the stream extraction operator (>>) much like we've done before with **cin** but instead use it with **fstream** or **ifstream**.

It's also done like so:

```
char data[100];
f >> data;
```

Note: Reading like this will read all data up until a space or newline

Working example

Above is all you need to know to read a write to a file, below is working code example with reading and writing:

```cpp
#include "stdafx.h"
#include <iostream>
#include <fstream>

using namespace std;

int main()
{
        //Opens a file for writing
        fstream write;
        write.open("file.txt", ios::out);

        //Writes data to file
        write << "Example Data" << endl;
        write << "More example data" << endl;

        write.close();



        //Opens a file for reading
```

```
        fstream read;
        read.open("file.txt", ios::in);


        //"!read.eof()" = Read while not end of file
        //.eof() is a bool to flag if the end of the file has been reached
        char data[100];
        while (!read.eof())
        {
                //Reads in
                read >> data;

                //Prints
                cout << data << endl;
        }


        read.close();
}
```

Output

>Example

>Data

>More

>example

>data

As you can tell, each read command is stopping when it reaches a space or a newline (as mentioned above), in this case it just complicates the read section because now we have all the sentences separated. One way we can fix this is by using "getline()", We'll adapt the above example to read whole lines, changes will be highlighted:

```cpp
#include "stdafx.h"
#include <iostream>
#include <fstream>
#include <string>

using namespace std;

int main()
{
        //Opens a file for writing
        fstream write;
        write.open("file.txt", ios::out);

        //Writes data to file
        write << "Example Data" << endl;
        write << "More example data" << endl;

        write.close();




        //Opens a file for reading
        fstream read;
        read.open("file.txt", ios::in);
```

```
//"!read.eof()" = Read while not end of file
//.eof() is a bool to flag if the end of the file has been reached
string data;
while (!read.eof())
{
        //Reads in
        getline(read, data);

        //Prints
        cout << data << endl;
}

read.close();
}
```

Output

>Example Data

>More example data

The <string> library has been included as to access the getline() method, this method uses the "read" stream as the first parameter and the second parameter being the place for the data to be stored. As you can tell "data" has also been adapted to a string, this just allows a cleaner way of reading in because we don't need to specify length.

Recursion

A recursive function is a function that contains within its definition a call to itself, this therefore creates a loop and if you're not a carful an infinite one.

Recursion can be very useful as it creates iteration with a small code base, below is a recursive example:

```cpp
void Recursive(int count)
{
        if (!(count <= 0))
        {
                //Prints current value of count
                cout << count << endl;

                //Makes recursive call
                Recursive(count - 1);
        }
}
```

All this function does is count down from the initial value that's it's called with, so:

```cpp
Recursive(5);
```

Will output:

```
>5

>4

>3

>2

>1
```

The key bit about the function above is the if statement, this makes sure that recursive call stops, this is known as the stopping condition as stops the program from crashing due to overflowing function calls.

A more useful example that you'll see everywhere if you're researching recursion is a factorial example, for anyone that needs refresh a factorial is the product of all the positive integers from 1 to a given number, so the factorial of 4 (written like 4!) is:

```
4! = 4 * 3 * 2 * 1 = 24
```

And the recursive code looks like this:

```
int Factorial(int value)
{
```

```
    if (value > 0)
    {
            return value * Factorial(value - 1);
    }
    else
    {
            return 1;
    }
}
```

As you can see there is a function call in a return statement, you'll use this a lot in recursion as it means the function will fall into sort of like a recursive whole, hit the bottom (in this case "return 1") and use this information at the bottom to fill in the gaps on the way up and determine an answers back at the top. This all gives a different way to deal with iteration in a clean concise way.

Exercise

This is a hard exercise and it aims to try and trigger a good understanding of recursion, so take your time and do some background research prior to starting. In this exercise I would like you to create a recursive function that calculates Fibonacci's sequence with all the values below 1000, printing them as you go.

Start it off with a call like so:

```
Fibonacci(0, 1);
```

Note: You'll need two parameters, previous and next.

Solution

Something similar to this:

```cpp
#include "stdafx.h"
#include <iostream>
using namespace std;

int Fibonacci(int previous, int next)
{
    //Print
    cout << previous << endl;

    if (next < 1000)
    {
        int newNext = previous + next;

        return Fibonacci(next, newNext);
    }
}
int main()
```

```
{
    Fibonacci(0, 1);
}
```

Output
> 0
>1
>1
>2
>3
>5
>8
>13
>21
>34
>55
>89
>144
>233
>377
>610
>987

Remember there are always different ways of doing things, so if you got the same output it's still correct!

Pre-processors

Are just instructions for the compiler to process before any code is complied, they all begin with a (#) and do not end with a semi colon (;) as they are not statements.

#define

Define is used to create a definition of a symbol or word, the most common example is using #define to specify if the program is in debug mode, this allows you to only run debug code when the debug flag is defined. You can also use them to define constant no-changing values, an example is below:

```
#include "stdafx.h"
#include <iostream>

#define NUMBER 10

using namespace std;

int main()
{
```

```
        cout << NUMBER << endl;
}
```

Output

>10

This is used as kind of an alias system, not variable is defined here but you can put very important values in these define statements and create more readable code.

You can also use #define statement to create macro-functions, it is done like so:

```
#define BIGGEST(a,b) ((a < b) ? b : a)
```

This is effectively saying if b is greater than (<) a return (?) b as the value else (:) return a.

And is called like any other function:

```
cout << BIGGEST(10, 2) << endl;
```

One of the most useful real world uses of this would be to create a better syntax for a for loop within the #define, this is just for syntax purposes:

```
#define For(index, max) for(index = 0; index < max; index++)
```

All this does is just define a for loop within the #define body, you just put the list and the value you want to index and you then have a tidy syntax.

I looks like this when used:

```
int i;
For(i, 10)
{
        cout << i << endl;
}
```

Much nicer than the equivalent:

```
for (int i = 0; i < 10; i)
{
        cout << i << endl;
}
```

Please note these do the **exact** same thing, it's just a different syntax.

Conditional Compilation

This is used in conjunction with the #define, there is **#ifdef** (If defined) and **#ifudef** (If undefined) that both check for #define statements. It can be used like:

```
#ifdef VERBOSE
        cout << "Print!" << endl;
#endif
```

It surrounds code and say for example there is not a #define above the code will be ignored.

```
#define VERBOSE;
```

#ifudef is just the opposite and will ignore code if there is a #define.

The # and ## operators

The # operator replaces a macro with that given string, and example is below:

```
#define CREATE_STRING(x) #x;
```

Then when it's called it will be replace the entire call with "x", so:

```
#include "stdafx.h"
#include <iostream>

using namespace std;

#define CREATE_STRING(x) #x

int main()
{
    cout << CREATE_STRING(STRING EXAMPLE) << endl;
}
```

Output

>STRING EXAMPLE

This is because:

CREATE_STRING(STRING EXAMPLE)

Calls:

#define CREATE_STRING(x) #x

Where:

```
#define CREATE_STRING(STRING EXAMPLE) #STRING
EXAMPLE
```

And

```
#STRING EXAMPLE
```

Is equal to:

```
"STRING EXAMPLE"
```

Operator

The double hash operator concatenates two items into one, this is better explained with an example:

```
#include "stdafx.h"
#include <iostream>

using namespace std;

#define MAKE_ONE(a, b) a ## b

int main()
{
```

```
        int numone = 100;

        cout << MAKE_ONE(num, one) << endl;
}
```

Output

>100

Why has this happened? Let's walk it through:

The double hash takes two items and concats them so:

```
MAKE_ONE(num, one)
```

Resolves to:

```
#define MAKE_ONE(num, one) num ## one
```

And;

```
num ## one
```

is equal to:

```
numone
```

So:

```
cout << MAKE_ONE(num, one) << endl;
```

Equals

```
cout << numone << endl;
```

And the variable above is called and the output is 100.

Dynamic memory and pointers

To understand pointers you need to understand how variables are stored. Variables are allocated a memory location, and the size is dependent of the size of the variable. A pointer is a variable that holds the address of that location, so it allows direct access to a variable.

A pointer is defined like so:

```
int* p;
```

You then need to assign the pointer to point at an actual memory location, to do this we need to use the reference operator (&). The code below assigns a variable for the pointer to point at:

```
#include "stdafx.h"
#include <iostream>
```

```
using namespace std;

int main()
{
        int i = 10;
        int* p = &i;
}
```

This defines a pointer to an integer, lets print out the value just after initialisation and see what it looks like, by adding the code below to the bottom of the body of the main method:

```
cout << p << endl;
```

Output

> 008FF768

This is the address that holds the integer "I"

Note: This value will be different every time

This allows you to pass values by reference, if you were to pass the pointer as a parameter any changes to the pointer will result in a change to the base variable, the example below demonstrates this:

126

```
#include "stdafx.h"
#include <iostream>

using namespace std;

void Change(int* pointer)
{
        *pointer = 200;
}

int main()
{
        int i = 10;
        int* p = &i;

        cout << "Before: " << i << endl;

        Change(p);

        cout << "After: " << i << endl;
}
```

Output

>Before: 10

```
>After: 200
```

As you can tell the value of "I" has changed but without the direct changing to the variable.

Pointers can point to any data type, you can even have pointers to objects.

New and delete operators

The **new** operator allows manual allocation of memory for a data type, see the example below:

```
double* p = new double;
```

As you can tell the **new** keyword allocates memory and returns a pointer to that memory, in the case of the example above it's a pointer to a double, this is manually allocated memory and the compiler will not manually release the data and if this isn't manually rectified there can be what is called a **memory leak** where memory is taken up unnecessarily.

This is where the **delete** operator comes into use, this is the opposite to the **new** keyword and will deallocate the memory for the variable.

Let's put the operators into work:

```cpp
#include "stdafx.h"
#include <iostream>

using namespace std;

int main()
{
        //Creates pointer
        double* p = NULL;

        //This checks to see if memory has been allocated
        //It just checks to make sure "p" is pointing to something
        if (!(p = new double))
        {
                cout << "ERROR: Memory problems" << endl; //Will
only print if there is a problem
        }

        //Changes value etc
        *p = 100;
        cout << "P is: " << *p << endl;

        //Deallocates memory
        delete p;
}
```

As you can see there is a check for the allocation of memory for p, this is a recommended practise because it keeps tabs on any memory problems, if you were to just do this:

```
double* p;
p = new double;
```

If the second line was to fail p could be pointing to any memory location and would cause a crash if the value of p was changed.

Dynamic memory for arrays

As you can do with variables, you can also do with arrays with the:

- **new[]** to allocate a chunk of memory

- **delete[]** to deallocate chunks of memory

So for example if we wanted to make an array of pointers to 5 objects:

```cpp
#include "stdafx.h"
#include <iostream>

using namespace std;

class MyClass
{
public:
        MyClass()
        {
                cout << "Made!" << endl;
        }
        ~MyClass()
        {
                cout << "Deleted!" << endl;
        }

};

int main()
```

```
{
    //Create
    MyClass* classes = new MyClass[5];

    //Delete
    delete[] classes;
}
```

Output

>Made!

>Made!

>Made!

>Made!

>Made!

>Deleted!

>Deleted!

>Deleted!

>Deleted!

>Deleted!

As you can see the first line in the main() creates 5 MyClasses, the constructors fire and print "Made!", the next link then goes onto free the memory the destructors fire and print "Deleted!", this can be used to create a lot of pointers with a very small amount of code.

Pointer arithmetic

You can add a value onto a pointer to move it along to the next memory location, let's say we have a pointer to an integer, and on a 64bit system an int should be 4bytes. So:

```
int* p = new int;
p = p + 1;
```

The code above will move to the next 4 bytes, by "+1" you say move to the next variable sized gap, so for example if we had a "long long" that should be 8 bytes adding one will move 8 bytes along. You can also do this in the opposite direction and take away one, this does the exact same just in the other direction.

The example below demonstrates this:

```cpp
#include "stdafx.h"
#include <iostream>

using namespace std;

int main()
{
    //A size check
    cout << "int is: " << sizeof(int) << " bytes" << endl;

    //Creates memory
    int* next = new int[10];

    for (int i = 0; i < 10; i++)
    {
        //Moves along 4 bytes
        cout << next + i << endl;
    }

    //Deletes memory
    delete[] next;
}
```

Output

>int is: 4 bytes

```
>00DDDB50

>00DDDB54

>00DDDB58

>00DDDB5C

>00DDDB60

>00DDDB64

>00DDDB68

>00DDDB6C

>00DDDB70

>00DDDB74
```

As you can see, memory is allocation and the pointer is moved along by 1 each time. As you can see from the output the hexadecimal addresses are 4 different from each other because the memory addresses are adjacent.

End of chapter Quiz

1. What does the flag "ios::app" mean?

2. Why is it important to close a file?

3. Which operator is used to writing data to a file?

4. What does .eof() signify?

5. What does every recursive function need?

6. What does #ifudef mean?

7. What does the "##" operator achieve?

8. When should "delete []" be used?

9. What does the "new" operator return?

10. What does adding 1 to a integer pointer?

Answers

1. It will open the file in append mode.

2. It releases resources attached to the file.

3. Insertion operator (<<).

4. Is a method that returns true when the end of the file is reached.

5. A stopping condition to prevent endless looping.

6. Will include the code it encapsulates if the alias is undefined.

7. It concatenates and replace two values.

8. When you want to delete a block of user assign memory.

9. A pointer to a newly created memory location

10. If the integer is 4 bytes it will move along 4 bytes.

www.ingramcontent.com/pod-product-compliance
Lightning Source LLC
Chambersburg PA
CBHW071216050326
40689CB00011B/2336